I WISH
EVERYONE WAS AN IMMIGRANT

The 8 Traits Successful Immigrants Have,
and How You Can Use them
in Your Pursuit of the American Dream

PEDRO MATTOS

Copyright © 2018 Pedro Mattos.
All rights reserved.

No part of this publication may be reproduced, distributed, or transmitted in any form or by any means, including photocopying, recording, or other electronic or mechanical methods, without the prior written permission of the publisher, except in the case of brief quotations embodied in reviews and certain other non-commercial uses permitted by copyright law.

ISBN: 9781729463628

I would like to dedicate this book to the following people:

Mom: You both are the reason why I wrote this book.
Mom, your sacrifices allowed me to live the life of my dreams.
You are my superhero.

Colleen: Thank you for being my biggest supporter, editor, and best-friend. There is no way I would have accomplished the feat of writing this book without you.

The Self Publishing School Team: You all changed my life completely. I honestly could not be more grateful for all of the opportunities that you have given me. Can't wait to continue to impact lives with you guys. The best is yet to come!

NOW IT'S YOUR TURN

Discover the EXACT 3-step blueprint you need to become a bestselling author in 3 months.

Self-Publishing School helped me, and now I want them to help you with this FREE WEBINAR!

Even if you're busy, bad at writing, or don't know where to start, you CAN write a bestseller and build your best life.

With tools and experience across a variety niches and professions, Self-Publishing School is the only resource you need to take your book to the finish line!

DON'T WAIT

Watch this FREE WEBINAR now, and Say "YES" to becoming a bestseller:

bit.ly/2ELozyd

TABLE OF CONTENTS

Introduction	1
1 Delayed Gratification	13
2 Putting others first	19
3 Work	31
4 Always be Positive	45
5 Be Unrealistic	51
6 Take Risks	59
7 Don't Listen to Rejection	71
8 Gratitude	91
Conclusion	95

INTRODUCTION

The Immigrant Hustle

My mentor, Kami, and I had been working on this house for about two weeks.

I was at the tail end of running a successful painting business after my freshman year at the University of Massachusetts, and, by that point, all I wanted to do was collect my final check and never touch a paint brush again.

It was a Sunday, and Kami had to leave early in order to make it to catch a flight back to her home in Michigan. I was alone and tasked with putting the finishing touches on one of my last projects of the summer. Lucky for me, working on Sundays was no strange task. In fact, I don't think I had taken a single day off from building my business.

I have always been labeled a "hustler." I have never been the smartest nor the most talented, but what I do have is an inner drive that pushes me to put in more hours than others.

I like to call that trait "the immigrant hustle." All of us who have made the move to a new country have it, and it is present in our daily actions as we strive to pursue our own version of the American Dream.

* * *

It was January 2005, and I was six years old. My mother told me that we were moving our comfortable lives from Belem, Brazil, to start fresh in Orange, Massachusetts. I was extremely confused; nothing was broken, so why fix it?

We lived on the third floor of a beautiful high-rise. This place had everything six-year-old Pedro could possibly want. There was a soccer court in the backyard, two pools, plenty of space to play hide-and-seek, and best of all, five of my closest friends were just an elevator ride away. I loved my life, and I saw no reason why it had to change. Unfortunately, no crying or arguing would change my mom's mind.

On June 19, 2005, I said goodbye to my family and friends and embarked on a journey that would officially kick off my life as an immigrant. My mindset started to change when I realized all the possibilities that came with the move. I started to think about finding a soccer team. Sports have always been an escape for me. They were something I could pour my all into and forget about the world outside. I could see myself becoming the best soccer player in the United States. Whether or not that was realistic, it gave me something tangible to strive for. I knew there were going to be challenges, but I was ready to face them head-on and eventually come out on top.

There were many ups and downs for our family in the first year and every year after (details coming soon), but what I know now as a wise 20-year-old is that many of the challenges that my family and I faced are shared by millions of folks who have chosen to take the immigrant path as well.

Ever feel misunderstood because your accent was just "too strong"?

Ever get laughed at for eating food in a way that is not common to those around you? (I still think that the Americans are the weird ones for not putting ketchup on pizza!)

Ever cry on the phone while talking to a sibling or parent, not knowing if you are ever going to see them again?

Ever feel so distant from the world outside of your four walls that, even if you tried, you don't think you will ever be accepted by those around you?

Ever take a job that you are overqualified for because laws and regulations won't allow you to practice your trained occupation?

Ever sit around and dream about having one meal that you know won't taste right unless you are in your native home?

Ever feel like you just need to go back home?

I know you do. Trust me, I do too. I could go on forever about specific pains that relate only to us immigrants.

But I could also go on forever about all the lessons that we have learned and how we can use those lessons to achieve any goal that we set. I believe immigrants are modern-day superheroes equipped with powers that can never be taken away from us once they are obtained.

Don't believe me? Just take a look at this list of people that have utilized their immigrant superpowers to accomplish incredible things:

Steve Jobs – CEO/Founder of Apple Inc.
Elon Musk – CEO/Founder of Tesla / SpaceX
Steve Chen – YouTube
Sean Rad – Tinder
Sergey Brin – Google
Travis Kalanick – Uber
Jan Koum – WhatsApp
Max Levchin – PayPal
Mike Kreiger – Instagram
Arash Ferdowsi – Dropbox
Andrew Grove – Intel
Phil Libin – Evernote
Pierre Omdiyar – eBay
Jerry Yang – Yahoo
Sanjey Mehtora – SanDisk
Andrew Viterbi – Qualcomm
Ray Kroc – McDonald's
William Colgate – Colgate
Tomer London – Gusto
Patrick Collison – Stripe
Ragy Thomas – Sprinklr
Christian Gheorghe – Tidemark
Renaud Visage – Eventbrite
Igor Sikorsky – The first successful American helicopter
Charles Wang – Computer Associates
Adam Neumann – WeWork
Nine of our Founding Fathers
Nigel Morris – Capital One Financial Services
Alexander Graham Bell – AT&T
William Russell Grace – W.R. Grace & Company
John W. Nordstrom – Nordstrom
Helena Rubinstein – Helena Rubinstein, Incorporated
Marcelo Claure – Brightstar
Daniel Aaron – Comcast Television Company
Gary Vaynerchuk – VaynerMedia

Renaud Laplanche – Lending Club
Marcus Goldman & Samuel Sachs – Goldman Sachs
Dhiraj Rajaram – Mu Sigma Inc.
Noubar Afeyan – Joule Unlimited
William Procter – Procter & Gamble Co.
Mario Schlosser – Oscar Health
John Collison – Stripe
Tien Tzou – Zuora
Elizabeth Arden – Elizabeth Arden, Inc.
Ayah Bdeir – littleBits
Liz Claiborne – Liz Claiborne, Inc.
Charles Pfizer – Pfizer
William Mow – Bugle Boy Industries
K.R. Sridhar – Bloom Energy
Ben Huh – Cheezburger
James L. Kraft – Kraft
Andy Bechtolsheim & Vinod Khosla – Sun Microsystems
Peter Weijmarshausen – Shapeways
Maxwell Kohl – Kohl's
Michelle Zatlyn – Cloudflare
Nathan Cummings – Sara Lee
Kevork Hovnanian – Hovnanian Enterprises
Phil Jaber – Philz Coffee
Iqram Magdon-Ismail – Venmo
Jeong Kim – Yurie Systems
E.I Du Pont – DuPont
Andrew Carnegie – Carnegie Steel Company
James Gamble – Procter & Gamble Co.
Beto Perez – Founder of Zumba
Alexander Asseily – Jawbone
Chamath Palihapitiya – Social Capital
Arianna Huffington – The Huffington Post

Read more about these immigrant superheroes at bit.ly/2yIXAOy and bit.ly/2AAViT6.

These people have built incredible companies, created millions of jobs, added billions of dollars to the American economy. They all started with one thing: a dream and life experiences that gave them the edge that they needed to make a great impact.

I believe there is an extra gear inside the brains of all of these immigrants. Because of our similar challenges, I think we come out on the other side having learned lessons and skills, that, if utilized, can drastically increase our chances of getting what we want out of life. This extra gear allows immigrants to willingly take risks and endure years of patience. I like to frame it as our "unfair advantage," and, in this book, I will lay out eight lessons that ALL immigrants have learned by going through the common challenges that come with trying to establish oneself in a new country.

My goal in sharing these eight lessons is to remind YOU that, even though you might be struggling immensely right now, or thinking about calling it quits and packing your bags to go back home, it will all be worth it in the end because you are becoming a person that will have an unfair advantage in every aspect of life.

Being an immigrant is a blessing! Always remember that!

A Message

Now, at this point, you might be thinking, "Okay, it would make sense if someone like Andrew Carnegie, one of the world's wealthiest men of all time, wrote this book, but who are you? Are you a successful entrepreneur? Have you achieved everything that you want out of life? Are you really even an immigrant?"

First of all, yes. I am an immigrant.

Second of all, no. I am not a successful entrepreneur. I have not yet achieved everything that I want out of life (which would be weird if I had, because I am only 20 years old at the time of this writing).

Who am I, you ask? The answer to that question can go a few different ways. I would say that, depending on who you compare me to and in what area of life, I am both extremely successful, having accomplished great feats, and considered an epic failure, with no direction or sense of reality. Both of the above statements about me are correct, and I would say that this is true for you as well. We are all successes and failures in life. The question really becomes "compared to what?"

I am not writing this book with a sense of authority. I don't see myself as "Zen-like" or one that has the secret key which, if used, can open the door to all things successful. What I am, however (and I think that this is more important than any amount of wealth that I could accumulate), is fulfilled.

I can honestly say that I have been on a great streak of waking up every day and feeling blessed with the life that I have been given, and in that sense, I think that I am a successful man.

My fulfillment did not happen overnight, and that is the reason I am writing this book. I can attribute that success to the eight lessons that I could only have learned by living my life: the life of an immigrant. My hope is that at least one person will change the way that they think about their lives and find peace and fulfillment as well.

One of the reasons that I felt the responsibility to write this book is I know of one person who absolutely needs to read it. That person is my mother.

Let me explain:

When most people think of the typical "coming to America story," they usually think of someone escaping poverty, fleeing from a war zone, or any other multitude of extremely tragic scenarios. My mother's story doesn't fall under any of those scenarios. In fact, my mother lived quite a comfortable life as a pediatrician in Brazil. We had maids and a cook. My mother had a car (which is an extreme luxury in Brazil) and a nice apartment near downtown Belem. I was going to a respected Catholic school, and life seemed to be going as well as it could have been.

My mother, however, wanted to ensure that my sister and I were set up in an environment that had an endless number of possibilities. The education system, the safety, the relatively stable government and economy of America were all great selling points for my mother. Those, along with the fact that she had met my stepfather, who happened to be an American, led to the ultimate decision to make the move.

I can't say how my mother actually felt about it all. I am sure that fear and uncertainty were some of the most prominent emotions during the months and weeks leading up to the move. I can't imagine what it would have been like to leave a life that took 40 years to build.

Sometimes, as human beings, I guess we are always searching for a better opportunity. The grass always looks greener on the other side, and we are always thinking about the "what-ifs" and better alternatives to our current realities.

You never realize how good you have it until life takes it away. I think my mother learned this the hard way.

Fast-forward 13 years after we first set foot in America, and my mother is still struggling with the idea that her situation is actually a blessing in disguise.

In her eyes, she has not achieved all that she had wanted to on her journey. The initial hope of becoming a doctor quickly went down the drain. After that, years of confusion mixed with layers of frustration and depression followed.

Honestly, I couldn't care less if she is the only person to read this book. However, I know there are many people out there in a situation similar to hers, so, if this book can help her, it may be able to help someone else. Even if it is just one other person.

* * *

I can only imagine how my mom felt throughout those years. There were many days she spent sleeping because only in her dreams was she away from the disappointing reality she was facing.

There were many days my mother spent crying because only in tears could the feelings so deeply hidden in her soul be set free.

There were many days my mother spent contemplating whether she had made the right decision. Honestly, I cannot say whether or not it was.

Mom, if you are reading this … I am sorry.

I am sorry for telling your story to the world.

I am sorry if you are reading this and don't understand how my writing this will be of any benefit to anyone.

Mom, I want to tell you one thing, I am writing this book for you.

That's right … I am writing this book for you and for anyone else who is in your position.

I am writing this book for those who have made one of the most difficult decisions a person can make: the decision to leave everything they have ever known and start over in an unknown land with the hope of providing a better life for themselves or their children.

I am writing this specifically for those times when you are laying in your bed and asking yourself why you made the decisions that you did.

I am writing this to encourage you and let you know that your investment in your future is already paying back dividends.

I am writing this because I want you and those in your position to realize that you are blessed, even though sometimes it isn't always easy to see how blessed you are.

I am writing this because I love you, Mom, and I wanted to thank you for everything you have done and sacrificed for me.

* * *

So what exactly will you be getting from reading this book other than a pep talk?

Great question. I am not a fan of motivational speeches myself.

What I will do instead is outline eight lessons I believe all immigrants learn from the time they leave their home country to the time they eventually find their place in a new country.

What makes this book different from others that tell you how to live your life and achieve great success is that I am not teaching you anything you don't already know.

Because of the similar experiences that we immigrants have faced, we have already learned these lessons. If you are an immigrant, you already have the tools that you need.

There is power in having to learn a new language in a completely unforgiving environment. The same is true for being an outsider in almost all circles you find yourself in when you are an immigrant. You learn a lot about yourself and life when you have no one around you who understands your situation outside of your immediate family. You gain great strength from fighting through the systemic obstacles that prevent you from having the rights that come with being a natural-born citizen.

In this book, I explain exactly what the lessons immigrants learn are, why and how every immigrant learns them, how I was able to apply them in my own life (and what happened when I didn't), and, most importantly, I will make sure you understand that being an immigrant is one of the greatest advantages you will ever have as you lead your life.

CHAPTER 1

DELAYED GRATIFICATION

Don't Order the Fries

Anyone who is familiar with the personal development world has heard of the term "delayed gratification."

The concept is simple, and, in a nutshell, delayed gratification describes the act of giving up short-term pleasure for long-term gain. We all understand this concept and apply it to our daily lives to some degree.

You choose not to order french fries and a milkshake, delaying the instant gratification of delicious food in exchange for long-term health. You decide to stay in on Friday night to study for a midterm exam, therefore passing up the instant gratification of spending time with friends in order to be able to ace the test. We have all acted upon this principle and know of its benefits.

Another way to think about this concept is through the framework called "orders of consequence." You can apply this framework by taking a decision and analyzing the effects of the decision at different points in the future.

Let's stay with the french fries and milkshake analogy. In this example, if you chose to order the french fries and milkshake, the first order of consequence would actually be positive! You would enjoy a tasty meal, and your taste buds would feel really good about it.

The second order of consequence, however, (the result of eating the fries and milkshake) is that you then feel bloated and maybe even a little sick depending on how much you eat.

The third order of consequence (which happens after repeatedly engaging in the activity described) is that you will gain unhealthy weight.

The fourth order of consequence is that you may not live as long or as well as you would have if had you made better food choices.

That was a very blunt example used to make a point. However, you can now see how a single decision can have multiple outcomes depending on when you choose to look back. By delaying gratification and pleasure in the first level of consequence, you set yourself up for better results than in the second, third, and fourth levels.

Delayed gratification is at the core of every decision made by those who choose the path of immigration. Most of the time, the beginning years an immigrant is living in her chosen destination prove to be more difficult than anything she's ever experienced before.

One can never really prepare for the difficulties that come with adjusting to a new culture. However, this is always done with an end goal in mind. A goal that, for the most part, proves to be worth it.

My mother is still waiting for the moment when she can say that the gratification she delayed has proven worth the struggle. I can't blame her, though.

Growing up, my mother lived a comfortable life. Living a middle-class lifestyle as the youngest daughter of a successful accountant (my grandfather) and a nursing professor (my grandmother), my mother enjoyed many of the privileges that Brazilians desire. As a child, her days were spent attending private schools, enjoying art lessons, and playing with dolls. Her weekends were often at our family-owned ranch about 30 minutes outside the city of Belem. This beautiful, paradise-like location gave my mother and her siblings the opportunity to experience nature while bathing in ponds and picking cocoa beans straight from the trees.

Upon graduating from high school, my mother decided to pursue a career in medicine. This was a path that was achieved through tremendous hard work and perseverance, which allowed her to continue the comfortable lifestyle she was accustomed to growing up.

During my first seven years on this planet, I reaped the benefits of the great choices that my mother had made career-wise. I did not worry about money or not having enough toys—heck, my lunch was even cooked every day by our own chef! It is unbelievable to think that someone would give that up for an opportunity to pursue an even "better life" by way of the American Dream.

My idol and inspiration for this book, Gary Vaynerchuk, has described the principle of delayed gratification time and time again when asked to describe his childhood. His story is a great example of an immigrant family that chose to delay gratification in order to achieve a much greater return in the end.

Gary and his family moved from the country of Belarus to the United States in the 1970s. Unlike mine, Gary's immigration journey was a result of his family desperately wanting to escape the communist regime that was in place in Belarus. Their motivation was purely out of survival, and they were willing to withstand whatever hardship came their way in America. They knew full well that it could not compare to the poor quality of life that they would have otherwise continued to lead in their home country.

The family first found themselves in New Jersey, where Gary's father, Sasha, worked as a stock boy and made two dollars an hour. Working diligently and saving every penny, Sasha clearly had a goal in mind, and he was not going to stop until he achieved it. He worked with the attitude that stocking shelves at a liquor store was a huge blessing, and that attitude led him to rise in rank at the store.

What's absolutely mind-blowing is that, in a five-year period, Sasha Vaynerchuk was able to go from stock boy to buying the entire store.

I can only imagine the long hours and sacrifice it took for him to be able to accomplish that goal. According to Gary, however, buying the store did not mean that his dad was now going to sit back and enjoy life. He had technically "made it" in the eyes of many, but Sasha had higher goals for himself and his family, and he continued to work endlessly throughout Gary's childhood to make his dreams a reality.

Gary Vaynerchuk is often quoted saying he didn't really know his dad growing up. His dad would go to work before Gary woke up and come home after he was in bed.

It wasn't until he turned 14 that Gary actually spent time with his father; however, that time wasn't spent on the baseball field or going to the movies. Instead, Gary was hired by his father to bag ice in the basement of their liquor store. This was a job that he would continue to do until he turned 17.

At 22, Gary became the co-operator of his father's liquor store, Wine Library, and was able to take the company from two to 60 million dollars per year through tremendous hard work and marketing expertise.

Gary has since gone on to become an absolute superstar in the world of social media and entrepreneurship. He currently runs VaynerMedia, a digital marketing agency that brings in over 150 million dollars in revenue per year. Gary also has successfully invested in companies such as Twitter, Tumblr, and Facebook, and has become a world-renowned personal brand, marketing, and overall business expert.

Gary has definitely inspired me to make many of the life decisions that I have made so far, and he was also a key factor in helping me realize what an advantage it was to be an immigrant in the country of the United States.

He really was the first person who put into words the extent to which immigrants delay gratification.

His father's story was just one example, but Gary himself showed enormous amounts of patience throughout his career. He has mentioned the fact that he basically saved all of his money during his 20s, with the goal to turn his savings into real wealth in his 30s.

What was the outcome?

Gary turned the hundreds of thousands of dollars he had saved into tens of millions through his investments.

This is delayed gratification.

My mother, as I write this, is still delaying her gratification.

She has still not reaped the rewards of the fruit she planted by coming to America. At least, she doesn't feel that she has.

There are no fancy cars in her garage, she did not achieve her goal of becoming a doctor in a foreign land, and her bank account has not grown over the last 10 years. So why do I think that delaying gratification was still an amazing move on my mother's part?

Well, I think that her season has just not yet arrived.

I think that there is light at the end of the tunnel for my mother. She just has not reached it quite yet.

With that being said, I would like to challenge my mother to look at her surroundings and look for signs of rewards that point to the fact that she, in fact, did make the right decision.

I would argue that the people my sister and I have become, as well as the person that you (Mom) have become through all of this adversity, are greater rewards than any of the materialistic items that I mentioned before.

I would like to promise one thing with that point. Your real gifts will soon be on their way, Mom, and your patience will be rewarded more so than you ever imagined … but keep in mind that it is not about what you will get as much as it is about who you will become.

CHAPTER 2

PUTTING OTHERS FIRST

Being patient is one of the major lessons that immigrants learn, and it is certainly one of the most important things that I learned over the course of my journey.

However, in order to have patience, you need to have a reason to be patient.

There needs to be a goal or a "why" that is so important to you that you are able to give up short-term pleasure for long-term benefits.

Talk to any immigrant, and I guarantee you that they did not choose to leave their home country solely because of their own self-interest. The prime motivation, the ultimate cause of the decision to immigrate, is almost always based on the fact that a person wants, more than anything else, to provide a better quality of life for his or her family.

My mother didn't choose to leave her great career and family because of her own self-interest. She wanted to make sure that my sister and I had the best opportunities to succeed. For my mother and many other immigrants, the best possible will always be the standard.

I fully believe that putting others first is a principle that we should all live by; the reason for this is that it is much harder to quit when someone else's life is on the line as opposed to your own. Even if it doesn't make sense at the moment, life will show you that putting others first is the right thing to do, over and over again.

The Chase

I have been chasing "success" for as long as I can remember.

My definition of success has changed almost as much as the seasons change here in New England; however, I am always chasing it nonetheless.

The chase began with the dream of being a professional soccer player after watching Brazil in the 2006 World Cup and ended after they got eliminated by France. It started back up again when I wanted to become the news anchor for SportsCenter and win a college scholarship to play soccer. Eventually, I decided that entrepreneurship was the most practical avenue to reach the level of success that I dreamed about. Today, I find myself in the process of learning the skills and the mindsets that it takes to become a successful entrepreneur.

This feeling of wanting to be a successful entrepreneur led to slowly starting small ventures while I was in high school. At first, it was your typical door-to-door landscaping business. By "landscaping," I mean asking the neighbors if they needed any yard work done, and doing it for them. Slowly, I started looking to start a business around something I enjoyed, which led me to begin both a soccer training business and an online handwritten letter business.

All of these ventures made me less than 1,000 dollars combined and were almost complete failures. However, I failed on my own terms, and that was something that forced me to get back up and start again.

As I went off to college at the University of Massachusetts, Amherst, my entire mentality was that I was going to start a business out of my dorm room. I majored in engineering, so I could meet a whiz kid who would help me launch the next Facebook, and, as soon as I set foot on campus, I was headed straight to the Entrepreneurship Club meetings.

During my first semester, as my time commitment towards classes continued to increase, my entrepreneurship drive steadily decreased. After my first semester of college, I went home with no business, which was a major disappointment.

Upon coming back from winter break, I was fired up and ready to start my dorm room business. My idea? Selling coffee and hot chocolate out of my room.

I had a purchased a Keurig coffee maker, 10 boxes of instant coffees and hot chocolates, made business cards, and created a marketing plan that was going to make Pedro's Coffees and Hot Chocolates a force to be reckoned with.

With my pockets filled with business cards, I headed to class on my first day back, excited about my prospects with my potential customers (classmates) and maybe learn a bit of chemistry, too.

Little did I know, this class would completely and forever change my entire life.

As I sat in the fifth row of this packed, 300-person lecture hall, I saw a blonde girl at the front of the class passing around a clipboard. Once it arrived on my lap, I read out loud the words: "Looking to make between eight and 10 thousand dollars this summer? Sign up to learn more about our internship opportunities with the Young Entrepreneurs Across America."

I proceeded to sign my life away that very moment.

Student Painters

Three days later, I found myself in the basement of the UMass Hotel, ready to attend an informational meeting about the internship with the Young Entrepreneurs Across America. I walked into that room as confidently as anyone, armed with the extensive business knowledge acquired through Gary Vaynerchuk YouTube videos and my own failed ventures.

I honestly thought, regardless of what business this Young Entrepreneurs company would help me start, that I would absolutely kill it.

Sometimes, being naive and having a positive attitude can be a good thing.

Soon after sitting down among six other students whom I did not think stood a chance against me in business, I started listening to a presentation being given by this short man from Michigan by the name of Aaron Acorn.

Aaron described how, in his first year with the Young Entrepreneurs, he ran an 80,000-dollar business and went on to run businesses worth over a million dollars by the time he graduated from Michigan State.

By that point, you could have given me three shots of espresso chased with four Red Bulls, and I don't think I could have been more hyped up. This had to be too good to be true.

Later on in the presentation, Aaron mentioned that the way he was able to run an 80,000-dollar business as a freshman and 1,000,000 dollars in business by the time he graduated was through the process of running an exterior painting business.

Half of the room was instantly turned off. Not even Aaron's joke, "So you guys didn't come to UMass for the great painting program?" could erase the fact that he proposed the idea that college kids who had never painted before could run five- and six-figure businesses doing just that.

Luckily, I was so mesmerized by the possibility that I could do something like that, I didn't care if I was selling painting services or hot chocolates. I was going to do this, and I was going to go all in.

* * *

Fast-forward to July 2017.

My business had gone through some ups and downs (more on those in later chapters), and, at this point, I had three employees on my painting crew and over 130,000 dollars in jobs sold but had only produced about 40,000 dollars.

I had a very interesting mix of workers, none of whom would be considered a "typical" student painters crew.

First, there was Sarah, 47 years young, who could climb a mean 40-foot ladder. Sarah had her ups and downs in life, but she was determined to get her life back on track. I was introduced to her through my stepfather, and we always had a laugh driving to work.

Then there was Mike, a 28-year-old, who was an amazing high-school athlete and had just moved back to our area after running a tree-removal company in Texas. Mike was sharp, a hard worker, and the leader of my crew.

Lastly, we had Trey, a 23-year-old, whom I used to play basketball with growing up. Trey had big dreams of becoming a rapper and making it big-time. For now, however, he was focused on putting food on the table for his family.

At first, the crew was doing great. We were beating budget, producing clean jobs, and making homeowners happy once they saw our final product.

However, as time went by, my production schedule was not moving at a pace fast enough to be able to finish all the jobs that I had sold … I just really needed more hands on deck.

That is when I received the phone call that would change the course of my summer.

Our team had about 10 hours' worth of work left on this yellow two-story house, and we were moving at a pretty decent pace, so I decided to get my crew some pizza. As we were waiting for our food to arrive, I received a call from a number whose area code I had never seen before.

I answered, "Hello, this is Pedro from Student Painters, who am I speaking with?"

A thick southern accent responded on the other side, "Hey Pedro! It's Mike, and I just moved here from Tennessee. I saw your flyer at the bar and was wondering if I could get an interview for the painting job. I've painted for over 20 years, so I know what I'm doing. Please just give me a chance, man."

At that moment, I thought that my prayers had been answered. The person who was going to take my crew to the next level had just given me a call. It did seem a bit of a red flag that he was finding my flyer at a bar, but hey, if he's good, I didn't care!

I answered, trying to set the right expectations with Mike and show authority, "Great, Mike! Thanks for the call! I would love to have you come out to the job site so you can show me what you've got. If it makes sense for you to continue after that, I will hire you. If not, I won't. Are you free this upcoming Saturday at 8 a.m.? We're going to be staining a deck in Athol. Also, just so you know, I pay 12 dollars an hour. Is that alright with you?"

Mike, with no hesitation, said, "Yes, sir! I'll be set and ready to go at 7:45. I promise you I will be the best painter that you have. I ran one of the largest painting businesses in Kentucky for years and have been painting since I was 12. You just need to give me a chance, man."

At this point, it seemed too good to be true. A painter with 20 years of experience, who ran his own business, wanted to work for a 19-year-old kid and make 12 dollars an hour? There had to be a catch.

Even if there was a catch, I didn't care.

I had a six-figure business to run.

* * *

He was, by far, the best painter on our crew skill-wise. His speed couldn't be matched, his steady hand while cutting trim and around front doors was firm, and he was very good at leading a crew. However, as I got to know more about Mike, it started to make sense why a 32-year-old man with 20 years of painting experience would be working for me.

In Mike's case, he had moved up to Western Massachusetts from Tennessee with his wife, Brittany, in search of a new beginning. They both struggled to get on their feet due to not knowing anyone in the area and trying to secure employment in a town that has been historically short on jobs. And their marriage was in a difficult place.

They were also struggling to find housing. We, thankfully, connected Mike and Brittany with Cliff, a local community leader, who opened his doors to him.

A rocky marriage wasn't the only shaky part in Mike's life. During our rides to and from work, Mike would tell me stories about his past, each time going a little deeper into how he ended up in the situation he was in.

He mentioned having a great business and making some pretty good money but then losing it all after the passing of his mother.

Mike turned to drugs and alcohol to cope with the pain, and that led him downhill fast. He eventually got arrested for possession of drugs as well as driving without a license and ended up leaving Tennessee as soon as he had the chance.

Seeing Mike struggle, yet keep a positive attitude, motivated me to try to help him out in any way that I could. He was working hard for me, and I was committed to helping him get back on his feet, and I wanted to help him start a successful business after I was done with my project for the summer.

After a couple of weeks, I started giving Mike potential job opportunities that he could pursue on the side when he wasn't painting for me. I knew that he needed the extra money, and I also was having to turn down jobs because I had sold so much already that I needed to focus on fulfilling my current contracts.

I tried setting the expectation that I would help Mike start his painting business as long as he kept his jobs to the weekends for the rest of the summer and focused solely on working for me on the weekdays. Unfortunately, the money he was making on the side jobs was bringing in way more than what I could pay him, and his motivation to work for me started to decrease.

I started to let Mike work on his own projects during the weekdays too, because he convinced me that he needed the money to pay rent and buy food. I really couldn't argue with either of those statements, so I let him do his thing.

The Truck

Throughout the entirety of the summer, one of my main problems was figuring out how to move my equipment from job to job. I had a small 2002 Mitsubishi Lancer that could barely drive me around, never mind all my stuff, so I had to improvise every time I needed to move my equipment and ladders to a different location.

As I was driving Mike back from one of our jobs one day, I spotted a truck that was within my price range and knew we had to check it out.

It was a green Ford from 1999, kind of run-down, but it definitely drove, which was a plus. I imagined the ease with which I would be able to move ladders if I bought that thing. Mike really liked the truck as well, and my plan was to actually sell Mike the truck after I shut down my painting business at the end of the summer.

After much negotiation and thought, I decided to buy the truck flat out. Mike chipped in a small percentage, so he could have access to the truck as well, and he promised that he would end up buying the truck once he was able to save enough money to do so.

Unfortunately ... this story does not have a happy ending.

I have not seen that truck in months.

Mike left town and took the truck with him.

He also stole about 300 dollars from Cliff, the older man who was nice enough to let Mike stay at his house for a very low cost.

My intuition says that Mike is back in jail at this point. There was no way he could have made it that far with no valid license or a lot of money saved up.

The interesting thing about the entire situation is that I felt strangely at peace throughout it.

I was out 2,000 dollars from buying the truck, my best painter was gone, and the person that I had tried to help out of a bad situation had completely turned on me.

However, I would do it all again.

A bad individual situation should never change the way that you look at life as a whole.

In most cases, the real beneficiary of the immigration journey is not the immigrant himself, but his children. Sometimes it is easy to let ourselves down, to not prioritize our own happiness, and to make decisions that will improve our own quality of life. However, when you attach your goals to a greater cause or to someone outside of yourself, you will find a level of motivation that you never knew you had. The downside of this occurs on the other side of the equation when the person or cause to which you have attached your goals disappoints you.

What if my mother's sacrifices had not thought me any lessons, and I had gone down a dark path? Would her effort be worth it?

At one point, I took accountability for helping Mike get to a better place in life. The fact that it didn't pan out in a way that equaled my expectations is irrelevant. One should give and put others first with no expectation of a return. I believe that putting others first is always the right thing to do. My mother showed me this through her choice to move and stay in the U.S. after many years of struggle. The least I can do is reciprocate her act of sacrifice to those around me regardless of outcomes.

Sometimes, we let single events change the way that we view the world. We think people are fundamentally bad because bad things happen.

I challenge you to continue to act in the self-interest of others, even if they let you down.

No.

Especially if they let you down.

CHAPTER 3

WORK

Effort is the greatest equalizer in the world.

What do I mean by that?

It's simple.

Effort is the greatest equalizer in a world where we are living in distinct circumstances, with a great diversity in wealth, resources, quality of life, talent, and an infinite number of other variables, in a world where our outside environment can and will affect the eventual outcomes of our journey (if we let it).

In this world, there is one thing that brings us all together. It is the number of hours that we have in a given day. The key differentiator among all of us is what we choose to do with those hours.

I have heard the term "immigrant hustle" being thrown around very often, especially in the entrepreneurial world.

This is basically the idea that immigrants have an extra chip on their shoulder, an extra motivating factor that allows them to go longer than anyone else at a given activity.

Gary Vaynerchuk has said that being an immigrant is one of the greatest advantages that you can have in this country because immigrants are willing to work for more hours than others, and the compounding effect of that sustained effort over a long period of time is the root cause that generated the massive list of successful entrepreneurs that we saw back in Chapter One. Not to mention all the other immigrants who went from zero dollars in the bank and zero connections to prospering in their chosen land.

So what is the point of this chapter? Everyone already knows that you have to work hard to succeed at anything you do. This isn't a revolutionary concept, so why bring it up?

Here's the thing ...

Although all of us know that working hard is a prerequisite to succeeding in anything we do, what most people struggle with is realizing that their actions need to match their ambitions.

This is the part where most of us struggle.

We think we work hard; we think we put in the hours necessary, but does that match our overall ambition? If we want to achieve more than 99% percent of the population, we need to ask ourselves if we are working harder than 99% of the population.

Hard work beats talent when talent doesn't work hard.

Replace talent with "wealth," "privilege," "intelligence," or any other variable, and the result will remain the same.

Figure out what your ambitions are and match your effort to those ambitions.

Hoop Dreams

Gary Vaynerchuk said that he worked *every single day* in his 20s.

Every one of them. No vacations, no holidays, no sick days.

Why? Because his ambition was to buy the New York Jets.

He wanted results that only a few people in this world can achieve, so he needed to outwork everyone else in the process to make it happen.

I have by no means achieved that level of sustained success in my lifetime.

I hope to use the principles I am writing about in this book to lead myself to achieve the goals that I have set, but I have certainly not achieved anything that the outside world would deem extraordinary.

However, in 19 years of roaming this planet, I have had two distinct ambitions for which I used this principle to outwork my competition and overcome my shortcomings to achieve the results I wanted.

Growing up, and still to this day, I have always been described as a "hustler."

To the outsider looking in, this may be a great thing, but to those who have been labeled this term, you know that being a "hustler" suggests that you are, more often than not, compensating for a lack of talent.

I cannot find a better way to describe myself on the basketball court, especially when I was starting out as someone who worked extremely hard and who had to compensate for an amazing lack of talent and athleticism.

I first touched a basketball on the Butterfield School playground before the beginning of fifth grade. At that point, I was fresh off of the plane from Brazil and looking to make friends any way I could.

I knew that wasn't going to happen through talking, as my English skills were subpar at best, and my sport of choice was soccer, which didn't seem to be a fan favorite at our school at the time.

I figured I'd give basketball a shot …

The playground was basically a wide blacktop court, with seven different basketball hoops evenly spread along the outside.

Further, the games that took place were very much segregated by skill and friend group. Having neither one of those personally, I was free to scope out the scene and use my underdeveloped interpersonal skills to find myself in a game. The really good kids would play half-court games on the 10-foot hoop on the far right-hand side of the blacktop.

Being competitive at heart, I figured I'd give it a shot going against the "good kids."

Lucky for me, I arrived just early enough where they were still picking teams, so I found myself in the first game, which was crucial because we only had a total of 20 minutes before classes started.

We decided to play four-on-four because there were eight of us there (how convenient), and the supposed two best kids would each pick teams.

My 4'6"-self was already expecting to be picked last, so that did not even faze me.

Sure enough, last pick I was, but, as my stepdad always says, "You know what they call the doctor who graduates last from medical school? A doctor." And with that attitude, I stepped onto the court, ready to compete.

Poised with a desire to prove myself, I decided to guard the other team's captain, Malik. I had met Malik earlier that summer, and we had ridden bikes and hung out a decent amount.

Right off the bat, I showed my stellar defense and hustle by guarding him very tightly ... maybe a little too tightly.

Malik did not appreciate my intensity and quickly shoved me off of him, accusing me of "riding" him as he dribbled. I just thought that's how defense was played.

Apparently, I was wrong, and the effort quickly made me an unpopular opponent on the playground.

I decided that basketball wasn't my thing after that day, at least until a couple of months later when winter arrived, and I realized that there was literally nothing else to do in Orange during the winter months other than to sign up for basketball. For the sake of escaping boredom, I decided to give the game another try.

My intention was to try out for the local travel team. The fifth-grade squad was coached by Brian Clark.

Brian was an absolute legend.

Mind you, when you are 10, anyone who can dunk and consistently hit a three-pointer seems like they should be in the NBA, but Brian was different.

To this day, 10 years later, I still don't know if I have played with anyone as good at the game of basketball as Brian Clark. The interesting thing is that he never played college basketball, and he actually only played one year of high school basketball due to his poor academic record. Apparently, he made a major life turnaround and was giving back to the community by helping develop the next generation of Orange hoopers. Little did he know, he would light a fire inside of me that would stay lit for many years to come.

Tryouts were rough, to say the least.

I remember not even knowing the difference between sneakers and real basketball shoes, and I was ice skating up and down the court with my slippery sneakers all night. I still did not know how to play good defense, so my opponents still hated me, and my wimpy arms could not generate enough power to get the ball to the hoop.

I did have one thing in my favor, however.

I lived in Orange, Massachusetts, which meant that there were barely enough kids at that tryout to form a team, which by default meant that I was automatically going to make the team.

Oh, the perks of living in a small town!

The winter season was one of the most embarrassing times of my life.

I barely played, my team won one game out of 10, and I finished the season with a total of two points. For you non-math majors, that means that I averaged .2 points per game. Phenomenal.

However, throughout that time, a funny thing happened.

Even though my season performance-wise was not great, I actually started to enjoy basketball.

I enjoyed going to practice and competing against other kids, every day seeing myself get a little better than I was before. I really liked the almost-instant feedback that I received after a period of consistent effort. On top of that, it was very easy to improve ... you just had to get to court and shoot.

After that season, I made the decision that I was going to be the most improved player on the team by the time tryouts arrived the following year.

Brian Clark, whom I mentioned earlier, gave me all the drills and techniques that I needed to work on my game. On top of that, my parents bought me a basketball hoop that we set up in my driveway. I had everything in place to become the next best hooper to come out of Orange, and that fire inside of me motivated me to go out and shoot jump shots every single day.

Looking back on it, I was obsessed about becoming a better basketball player. I worked out before school, read basketball biographies in class during reading time, watched YouTube highlights on some of the best players of all time, and was out on the driveway shooting and dribbling any chance I got.

I, honestly, have no memories of the summer of 2009 other than being out on my driveway and slinging jump shots. It was an absolute blast.

The routine was straightforward. Wake up, eat breakfast, and, at 8 a.m., start doing ball handling drills. I knew that I was small, so I needed to become a master dribbler to even have a chance at someday playing for the high school team.

I remember looking up dribbling drills by "Pistol" Pete Maravich, one of the top 50 NBA players of all time, and trying to imitate the ridiculous things he would do with the ball. Everything from behind-the-backs, through-the-leg dribbles, crossovers, two-ball dribbling, you name it, and I tried it.

After doing an hour or two of drills, I would set up chairs about 15 feet away from the basket, and I would start imagining real game situations. In those moments, I would pretend to be Michael Jordan or my favorite player at the time, Chris Paul. I would do move after move around the chairs and then pull up for a jump shot.

This little game would sometimes last for hours. I would be absolutely hypnotized, in a flow-like state, and, for those moments, there was nothing more important than making my next move and hitting my next shot.

As the days went on, my moves became tighter, my shots started going in more often, and my confidence as a basketball player kept increasing. Late at night, I would visualize what it would be like to start for our varsity basketball team in a few years.

Thinking about those days still gives me chills.

When sixth-grade tryouts rolled around, I was fully confident that I had accomplished my goal of becoming the most improved player on that team.

In fact, I was positive that no one had put in half of the hours or shot half of the shots that I had over the course of that year. Naturally, I thought that this was going to translate into on-court success.

Fast-forward three months ... I finished my sixth-grade basketball season with a total of six points.

All of that work ... all of those hours ... all of that effort and only six points to show for it.

It's hard to try to remember how you felt in a situation when looking back on it years later, but I imagine that "disappointed" and even "disgusted" are accurate descriptions.

I mean, it just didn't make sense how all of my effort refused to show results. I didn't understand how I could shoot so well in practice yet only score a total of three baskets during 10 games the entire year.

Maximum effort should yield immediate results.

Or so I thought.

Leaving It All on the Court

Think back to any situation in which you put your all.

You left absolutely zero in the gas tank. You exerted 100% of your energy into a certain activity.

Now, ask yourself if you received immediate benefits from those efforts. My best guess would be that the answer is "no."

That is a lesson that I didn't quite internally grasp at that time, but, over the years, I began to realize that the real key to effort is that it has to be combined with consistency over a span of time.

As immigrants, that might be years, sometimes even decades, until the fruit from our labor and sacrifice starts to reap. What I believe separates immigrants from others is the fact that we are willing to put in maximum effort over a longer period of time compared to those around us. This is an edge that I personally have not fully lived out yet. I haven't put in 20 years or more into any one cause in which I haven't seen the results from until the later years. I haven't been the one who saved every penny for decades, didn't buy a car for years, crammed a family into a small apartment, or spent years studying a difficult subject in a second language with the hopes of improving my quality of living. However, immigrant superheroes everywhere are doing those actions right now.

They do this because they have to, for their families and for their own sense of pride.

But they also put in maximum effort because they know that there is no alternative.

* * *

Unconsciously, I took that lesson and applied it to my situation as it related to the game of basketball.

I didn't want to let the effort that I put in go to waste, so I went into the off-season of my sixth-grade year with the same mindset as I had the previous year.

Throughout the years, I saw slow and steady yet consistent improvement.

You can call it a compound effect: consistent efforts that, over a long period of time, compound to show a major result.

In seventh grade, I scored 11 points.

In eighth grade, I scored 78 points, and I was, for the first time ever, a starter on the team.

In ninth grade, I scored 102 points, breaking triple digits for the first time in my career as the starting point guard for our high school's junior varsity team.

In 10th grade, I scored 116 points and made the varsity team, while also splitting time on the junior varsity team.

In 11th grade, I got my big break when Malik, the starting point guard for the varsity team and my arch enemy, tore his ACL during football season. That year, I scored 130 points and was the starting point guard on the varsity team.

In my senior year, Malik and I led our team to the playoffs as a backcourt duo that was a force to be reckoned with. I scored 156 points and finished my career with all-league honors and ended up being the winner of the Coach's Award for my team.

I pushed myself to the very limit every single year for eight years straight, trying to become the best basketball player that I could be. Looking back, I can honestly say that I left zero in the gas tank.

The question is … was it worth it?

Nowadays, about two years removed from my last game as a varsity basketball player, I can tell you that I do not remember the last time I touched a basketball or played in a pick-up game. Heck, I wouldn't even be able to tell you what team is the favorite to win the NBA championship.

From the outside looking in, it might seem clear that the amount of effort and time that I spent on basketball did not yield great returns. I mean, if I had played college basketball, even without a scholarship, that would be concrete proof that spending countless hours working on my skills was at least having some sort of impact on my life a couple of years later.

If you ever catch yourself thinking that maybe the effort and time you put into a specific area of your life did not generate the results that you had hoped for, I challenge you to take that belief and throw it in the garbage.

Frankly, if I were to go back in time, I would do all the same things over again. I would have spent just as much time, maybe even more, into honing my skills and pursuing mastery in the game. I take pride in knowing I was a good varsity basketball player.

Why?

Because the real benefit of pursuing one specific goal for a great period of time and putting maximum effort into achieving that goal is not the tangible result that comes when you reach the end of that pursuit.

The real benefit is *who you become in the process.*

Let me repeat that one more time … because it may very well be the most important lesson that you can get from reading this book.

By spending thousands of hours working on my basketball game, I became a person that could withstand the grind of pursuing mastery. I became a more patient person. I became a person that understood what it takes to be involved in the process of building something special for years.

No one can take that away from me, and no one will be able to take that away from you as well.

Gary Vaynerchuk spent 10 years building his father's company, Wine Library, from a two-million-dollar business to a 60-million-dollar business ... and left it with no significant money and zero ownership of the company. He basically started again from ground zero at the age of 30 after building a successful business.

I spent eight years of my life being completely committed and outworking everyone around me in the pursuit of being the best basketball player that I could be. I got zero athletic scholarship offers and never even had the chance to play professionally.

However, what happened to Gary and me during these pursuits is that we became different and better human beings.

Gary went on to invest in companies, such as Uber and Facebook, and to build a 150 million dollars per year revenue company called VaynerMedia. He did this because he had become a person who was capable of doing so by putting all of his effort into that first venture.

My life story is only getting started, but I envision a similar trajectory for myself, not so much in the sense that I am going to build a billion-dollar company, but in the sense that I will continue to put myself into better situations in my life because I became a person who could withstand years of working toward one goal.

When you are in a situation in which you have put in consistent effort over a long period of time but do not see the results that you wanted, first make sure that what you were working toward was actually what you truly desired. Ask yourself, "Am I a better person because I went through those experiences?" If the answer is "yes," you made the right decision all along.

Don't let the fact that you are not seeing immediate results stop you from outworking those who are around you.

However, if there is one thing that you can do to make the playing field equal, it is to focus on putting in more effort than anyone else.

If you do that, you will be okay in the end.

If you don't…well, the immigrant that is competing against you will.

CHAPTER 4

ALWAYS BE POSITIVE

What is the Alternative?

I have a serious question for everyone reading this book.

What is the alternative to having a positive attitude?

Now, you may answer that with the straightforward answer, "a negative attitude," and, if you did, you are technically correct.

My follow-up question to that is, "What is the purpose of having a negative attitude?"

I have yet to hear an answer to that question with which I can agree.

There is no upside to having a negative attitude. Period.

* * *

We all have an internal dialogue, a voice in our heads that is constantly narrating our daily lives and influencing the way that we think about situations.

Think about it this way.

You are driving down the road. It's rush hour, about 5:00 p.m. in downtown Boston, and you are looking to get yourself home as fast as possible.

You realize you didn't put on the right playlist when you first got in the car, so you quickly look down to check your phone and make sure that you have some combination of songs that aren't going to make your ride through traffic completely unbearable.

As you look up, going about 35 mph, you realize that the lights in front of you just turned red, so you slam on your brakes. You stopped in time, but unfortunately, the car behind you did not get the message, and you get rear-ended by a car that is going about 30 mph.

You think your day is now instantly ruined.

You quickly pull over into the nearest parking lot to check on the damage. At this point, you can't think about anything other than, "How much is this going to cost me?" or "How can I make sure that this idiot who hit me gets what he deserves?"

Congratulations, you have now put yourself in a negative state.

Notice I didn't say *the situation* put you in a negative state ... you were solely responsible for that.

"But the accident wasn't my fault! My car has major damage, and now I'm going to have to spend money that I don't have to fix this car! Don't I deserve to feel a little negative right now?"

"Isn't that normal?"

Reframing Your Thoughts

As an immigrant, there are a million ways that you can put yourself in a negative state or go through life with a negative attitude.

Think about how you will never speak your second language as well as those around you.

Think about how you will always be an outsider, both in the eyes of the law and in the eyes of your peers.

Think about how there are literally people out there, whom you'll never meet, who blame you and only you for the reason that they don't have a job.

Think about how much you miss your family and friends back in your home country.

Think about how hard it will be for you to get decent employment.

Are you feeling down yet?

If the answer is yes, why do you think that is? Did I make you upset? Did my statements give you a negative view of the outside world? If so, there lies your problem.

You see, your attitude, negative or positive, is always self-imposed. This means no matter what the situation outside of you is, the lens through which you choose to view the world is completely and one hundred percent under your control.

* * *

It's interesting how much your life can change in just a single day.

Let me rephrase that. It is interesting how much *your perception* of life can change in just a single day.

I would say that up to this point in my life, almost 20 years after my birth, the summer in which I ran a painting business was by far the most challenging time I have ever had to go through. The combination of long hours, stressful customers, challenging employees, and the constant mistakes that I made every single day took an immense toll on me. The fact that my home situation was extremely unstable on top of all that meant I was pushed to the very limit while trying to keep a positive attitude, even when outside factors made it almost impossible to do so.

It was during that difficult summer when the concept that I was in control of my attitude, no matter what the circumstances, became a vital aspect of my personality. Honestly, if I had not applied this lesson and ingrained this way of thinking into my brain, I guarantee that I would not have been able to make it out on the other side. If I hadn't made it through, I would not have had the multiple opportunities that came my way *because* of the fact that I did not quit when things got difficult.

At the beginning of this book, I listed many immigrants who went on to build extremely successful businesses that changed the world for the better. Imagine if any of them or their parents had let a negative attitude get in the way of their goals. They were able to, whether consciously or unconsciously, maintain a state of mind that allowed them to keep going. Just imagine what you can do when you realize that you, too, can control your attitude and mindset at all times, no matter the outside circumstances. I guarantee you that this lesson in itself will completely change your life if you let it.

* * *

One gloomy June afternoon, I sent my painting crew home and then went home myself after we realized that it probably would not have been the best idea to be painting in the rain. Soon after getting back to my house, I started to prepare myself for another session of placing hangers on doors across town (an unconventional, yet surprisingly effective marketing technique). I was in grind mode for my business and was working every waking moment to make sure that everything was running smoothly, while also trying to increase my sales and book more jobs.

However, before I was able to step out the door with my hangers, my mother told me that she needed to use the car to buy some groceries. I couldn't really argue with that, so I exchanged the couple hours of putting out door hangers for calling potential customers and customers from pending jobs, checking in with my mentor, and updating my sales and production spreadsheet.

About five minutes after my mother left, I got a call from her in which she expressed (great) concern about the way my car sounded. She described it as if something was dragging from the bottom of the car and rubbing against the road.

As I would later find out, that rubbing sound turned out to be just as bad, if not worse, than I had expected. Needless to say, I would not be driving my car for quite some time.

This incident just had to have happened at a time when a multitude of rainy days had forced me to push our production schedule back. Adding this to the fact that I had grossly underestimated the amount of time that it would take to complete two back-to-back projects, there was a perfect storm of madness within my business. At the same time, my bank account was continuing on a steady decline, which was only made worse by this car repair payment. I was in what my fellow Student Painters Executives call, "the panic zone."

Fast-forward to four days later. I remember sitting on my bedside writing (I actually decided to start a blog at pedrohmattos.com … you can check it out if you'd like) and feeling exponentially more calm, confident, and hopeful than I had just a few short days ago. Had I written the prior day as I had intended, I may have come up with a hopeful, yet frustrated story. Something along the lines of "I am not necessarily sure how I will get through this series of unfortunate events, but deep down I am still hopeful that the stars will soon align and I will figure out a way to keep moving forward."

However, as all entrepreneurs know … sales cure all. Just one day and 6,700 dollars' worth in sales later, I felt as if I was back on track. This is not to say that a couple of large sales fixed all of my problems, and this did not mean that by the next day I wasn't, once again, finding myself in the "panic zone." This does mean, however, that if all of these problems could be resolved, *all* problems can be resolved.

It is a skill to be able to look at situations for exactly what they are and not any worse or any better than what they are. That is a skill that I started to acquire then and that I continue to be aware of every day.

CHAPTER 5

BE UNREALISTIC

What Does It Mean to Be Realistic?

How does one conceptually know what is and what isn't possible within himself/herself?

One way we think will give us the answer is by looking at those immediately around us, gathering data, and making an assumption of our own worth and capability based on those findings. This, unfortunately, is the mindset that the majority of people have when deciding whether something that they are currently pursuing, or thinking about pursuing, is realistic.

"No one in my family makes 100,000 dollars per year. Why should I be able to?"

"No one from my high school has gotten accepted to an Ivy League school. How can I?"

"No one that I know has succeeded in business. Why should I?"

It's pretty easy to see how limiting those beliefs are, but they are still as common as dirt.

I know for a fact that I wouldn't have done any of the things that I'm proud to say I have done at this point in my life if I had limited myself based on what those around me were doing. Please take that into consideration the next time you find yourself asking if something you want to do is "realistic." It doesn't matter. You will never know until you try.

A better way to think about it is to think about the entirety of human existence and assume that a situation is realistic if, and only if, it has been done in the past. This idea has far more potential to influence exciting and meaningful decisions, as your idea of what is and what isn't possible is not constrained by looking at those around you.

However, I still believe that there are limitations to even this level of thinking.

For one, this method of thinking requires one individual to have knowledge of all events and situations that have occurred in the entirety of humanity. Although the Internet has given humans the ability to do some deep research on what has and hasn't been done before, it is still not comprehensive, and Internet research may lead to the inevitable side effect of lowering expectations.

For example, if there was an African-American boy in 2006 who wanted to find out whether or not it would be a realistic pursuit to try and become the president of the United States by doing a simple Google search of former African-American presidents, he would reach a disappointing conclusion.

"Why would I be able to become the president of the United States if no one who looks like me has been able to do so? That would be completely unrealistic!"

It's very easy to dismiss the occurrence of that scenario now. Most of us know that just two years after that little Google search took place, Barack Obama became the first African-American president of the United States. He set a precedent, therefore eliminating any beliefs from young African-American boys that said the dream of becoming the president was unrealistic. "If that first little boy had just waited two years, his dreams wouldn't have been crushed," we say. However, how many of us use that little boy's same way of thinking to stop ourselves from living out our dreams every day?

This leads me to my second critique of this way of thinking: Every single day someone does something that has never been done before.

This is another obvious thought when you think about it, but how many of us, once again, stop ourselves from doing what we really want to do because we don't know of anyone who has done it successfully before?

Thankfully, the world's greatest innovators did not have that mindset; otherwise, we would still be living in caves.

* * *

Immigrants, for the most part, *have* to think unrealistically just to earn their title.

Normally, an immigrant is the only one in his/her immediate circle to make such an unprecedented move. I know for my mother and me that was the case.

In my eyes, if you beat the odds and are able to find yourself in the great country of the United States, you have already accomplished one of the most statistically unrealistic goals out there. Just think of how many people around the world dream of having that opportunity, compared to how many make that dream a reality. I assure you that you'd be amazed by the answer to those questions.

*　*　*

I would go as far as to say that being "realistic" is a risk in itself. Limiting your expectations is the easiest way for you to reach all of your goals, but it's also the easiest way to never reach your full potential.

I believe that it was my expectations rather than my efforts that were the biggest factors in *limiting* the magnitude of my accomplishments.

Back to my painting business, although I would say that I left zero in the tank when it came to effort, I would also say that I did not set the bar as high as I could have when I first envisioned my goals for that endeavor.

I would like to once again make it clear that I was able to run an exterior painting business because I was mentored by individuals within a company called the Young Entrepreneurs Across America.

In order to land such an opportunity, I had to go through an interview process before being selected to make sure that I was qualified enough to handle the responsibility of running a business.

During this process, I was required to come up with a business plan of how I was going to go about running all aspects of the business and to outline what my ultimate revenue goals were.

To give some context, the average profit of those who "made it" (meaning the person running the business did not quit at any point throughout the summer) was about 50,000 dollars. There was also a reward trip for anyone who was able to bring in 70,000 dollars in revenue, and about one percent of all those who ran businesses hit the 100,000-dollar mark.

Once I was given that data, my eyes instantly went to that 100,000-dollar number. Just the thought of being able to do that seemed completely unimaginable for me at the time, even though others had done it in the past.

Looking back, I still don't understand what my train of thought was at the moment that I was making my business plan. Maybe I was feeling a lack of confidence in my abilities, or maybe I just didn't want to ruffle any feathers by stating that I was going to be one of the top one percent of students running a business that summer. Either way, in my business plan I stated that my goal was to run a 75,000-dollar business.

Man, did that come back to haunt me.

As it turns out, I produced almost exactly 75,000 dollars' worth of business at the end of the summer. A kiss of death if I had ever seen one.

The funny thing is that I had made almost double of that amount in sales, but wasn't able to deliver and ran out of time at the end of the summer. The universe has an interesting way of giving you exactly what you ask of it.

Sometimes, what you want (or think you can have) can be a dangerous thing.

Have you ever set a personal goal and then … hit it? Have you ever thought about what the results would have been if you had shot a little higher or dreamed a little bigger? Regardless, it is never a great idea to dwell on what could have been. We just need to remind ourselves to not make the same mistakes twice. Always shoot for the stars when pursuing goals and ventures, whether or not it seems realistic or possible.

The Payoff

On April 8th, 2018, I filed my taxes.

I got together with my good friend, Shawn, opened my laptop, and started going through the instructions laid out by H&R Block. As I looked through my W-2 forms, one thing, in particular, stood out to me.

The first form that I looked at was from Herrick's Inc., where I had made a total of 245 dollars during winter break of my freshman year in college, washing dishes and bussing tables. Once I saw that, I was completely taken aback. There is a saying that goes, "Men overestimate what they can do in one year, but underestimate what they can do in 10." If that is the case, I cannot wait to see what my life will look like in 10 years (if I continue to follow the rules I describe in this book).

The last year and a half since I last washed dishes at that restaurant has been an incredible journey.

I dropped out of school, started a painting business, ran marketing at a gym, received a job offer from a great company called HubSpot, turned down that offer to work under the CEO of Self-Publishing School, Chandler Bolt, and helped build the amazing company that is SPS, doing a job that I personally created. I have traveled to Cancun, New York City, Rio de Janeiro, Nashville, San Diego (where I ended up moving), Phoenix, Los Angeles, Detroit, San Francisco, Australia, Denver, and Boston, all for nearly free. I have seen some of my biggest idols, including Gary Vaynerchuk, Richard Branson, Michelle Obama, Daymond John, Simon Sinek, and Malcolm Gladwell, among others. I have dated my amazing girlfriend, Colleen, for two years, and our relationship is stronger than ever.

Life is an absolute blessing, and it has completely outdone any expectations that I could have set for myself as a college freshman working as a dishwasher.

The above statements are not to brag as much as to reflect on how quickly life can change for the better if you allow it to, if you are not held back by your limiting beliefs of what is realistic. When you dream big, plan, and execute, anything is truly possible.

Let this be your one shot of daily motivation.

Let this be a call to action for you to stop being held back by your own mind.

Be unrealistic, and life will show you that nothing is.

CHAPTER 6

TAKE RISKS

Dropping Out of College

If you were an investor and every decision that you made was the equivalent of buying an asset, how would you set up your portfolio?

Would you dump it all into volatile stocks? Or would you go for a safe alternative, and put your money into savings bonds?

My bet would be neither, right? The best investors have a diversified portfolio, and every investment decision is made by comparing and contrasting the potential outcomes and returns on that investment. If you actually want to have a chance at making some good returns, you better be willing to withstand the risk of potentially losing your upfront money, which, of course, is always a possibility.

In addition to the risk of losing money on an investment, there is also a risk that comes with not choosing a risky enough investment. This principle in economics is referred to as "opportunity cost," or the loss of potential gain.

When you decide that you are going to be unrealistic in the eyes of society and not sell yourself short by adjusting to the expectations of others, naturally you will start to make decisions which involve a certain level of "risk."

What society usually neglects to remember is the opportunity cost of not making that risky decision, a decision which could improve your life tremendously.

Thinking about the true costs versus the opportunity costs associated with the decision that my mother made in moving away from Brazil is mind-boggling.

I cannot say where I would be now had we not made the move, but I can almost guarantee that being even remotely involved in business would have been out of the question.

Writing a book before the age of 20? Not a chance.

Working for an amazing startup and enjoying what I do every day? Very unlikely.

Traveling with the same frequency with which I do now? Absolutely not.

Just considering those factors, the costs of not moving would have been immense based on what I would assume my life would look like had I stayed.

Now, for my situation specifically, it is very easy to see, looking back on a decision made 10 years ago, how all the cards played out in my favor. Pay attention to the keywords in that sentence: "10 years ago."

During the spring semester of my freshman year of college, I started to focus more and more on my painting business. This made it so that my time and energy spent on schoolwork naturally decreased.

I started to leave class more often to take phone calls with potential clients. I was using homework time to research videos on sales techniques, and I started reading books on mindset rather than on physics and chemistry. I completely blocked off my weekends to focus on my business, and as it got closer to the summer, that started carrying over into the weekdays as well.

All of a sudden, I started to really question for the first time my reasons for being in college.

I realized that I was doing well at this "business thing," and I was actually enjoying the process, even with all the difficulties that came my way. The same things could not have been said about what I was learning in the classroom. Lectures started getting harder to pay attention to because I was slowly but surely starting to realize that I just couldn't see myself becoming an engineer.

I have always been a hustler, in all facets of life. Naturally, that tendency carried over into my habits in the classroom, which meant that I spent an enormous amount of time in UMass' W.E.B. Du Bois library.

At one point during midterms of the second semester of my freshman year, I would routinely leave for class at 7:45 a.m., go straight to the library after class, take customers' phone calls in between assignments, and get back to my dorm between 12 a.m. and 1 a.m. every single day. That routine led to my taking naps in the back of lecture halls and my roommates thinking that I was completely insane.

I knew that this lifestyle could not continue. Something had to give.

Honestly, I didn't really have to think too deeply about the pros and cons of leaving college. There came a point when I just knew that I would be wasting valuable time and decreasing my learning potential if I stayed.

I had no idea what my next move was going to be, and I knew that I would not be running a painting business after the summer. However, I also knew there had to be a better way to continue to grow and to learn at a high rate.

Although I am a huge fan of doing things that involve risk, I did want to make sure that I had some type of plan if I was going to leave school.

I am someone who really enjoys putting himself in situations where my back is against the wall. The situations in which I literally have no other option but to figure it out are the ones in which I have always thrived. Knowing that, I made a decision that would put me in a situation where I either had to sink or swim. I made sure that if I made the decision to drop out, I was not even going to consider coming back. By doing that, I would have a sense of urgency to succeed that would force me to figure out my next step quickly.

I decided to purposely fail all of my finals. This meant that I would have no way of coming back to school unless it was through the community college route. I know, it sounds absolutely crazy and irresponsible, but the mindset of burning bridges and forcing oneself to succeed is one of the biggest reasons why immigrants so often find a way to make their goals a reality. In most cases, when you leave your home country … there is no turning back.

This is an extremely powerful position to be in.

I still haven't looked at my GPA for that semester … and I probably never will.

Once there was no turning back, I had to keep my eyes peeled for opportunities after the summer. I wanted to make sure that whatever I did would align with my ultimate goal of becoming an entrepreneur and maximizing my growth potential. I didn't just want to take any job that came my way.

One night, after a long day of sales and door-knocking, I was lying in bed on my phone, and I came across an article by Simon Fraser, who also ran a painting business and was a college dropout, about this college-alternative company called Praxis, that he was working for at the time.

Praxis' value proposition was to help young professionals kick-start their careers by teaching them valuable life skills and helping them to land an apprenticeship at a startup company. The "learn by doing" mindset that Praxis pushed completely aligned with what I was searching for. That, combined with the opportunity to work for a fast-growing startup without needing a college degree, proved to be the answer that I had been searching for all along.

After reading that article, I quickly took action and tried to connect with Simon Fraser. One reason is he was someone whose values aligned with mine. He created his own path, was not satisfied with following the status quo, and was dedicated to helping others find their way in the world. The second reason is I wanted to position myself in any way possible to land a spot in the Praxis program after the summer.

I read every piece of content they had, created a personal website (a project they take every participant through), made a value proposition, and reached out to past participants of the program.

By late June, I had decided that Praxis was going to be the initial next step for me after my painting business. I applied to become a part of the next incoming class in their program. I went through two rounds of interviews, wrote a few essays, and was feeling extremely confident during the course of the application process. The advisors seemed to like what I brought to the table, and I felt as if I clearly expressed how I could bring value to their community.

I did make one crucial flaw during the process, however. I sent over inaccurate phone numbers and emails for references, simply because I didn't double-check what I had written. I have always been a "big picture person" who tends to overlook details. The philosophy of "done is better than perfect" was something I referenced often. Unfortunately, being detail-oriented was a quality I couldn't be lacking during this process. Thankfully, the Praxis advisors let me know about the mistakes, I fixed them (or, so I thought), and sent back the references. I was quickly notified that, within a couple of days, I would be informed as to whether or not I had been accepted into the program.

As I mentioned earlier in the chapter, I am a huge proponent of taking a calculated risk. I also mentioned that I like to use a tactic of "burning bridges" as a tool to force me to succeed in certain situations.

In order to honor both of those principles (that I still do, and always will, live by), I decided to put the nail in the coffin and finally drop out of school.

I signed papers and all.

The day I knew I was supposed to find out about my acceptance into the Praxis program, I decided to head over to UMass' Admissions Office and officially resign. Interestingly enough, my girlfriend was also going to UMass that day, so I caught a ride with her. She had no idea what was about to go down.

As we drove down the highway on the way to the school, all I could think about was what I would say to the advisors, who were certainly going to try to convince me to think further about my decision. I started playing different scenarios in my head as to how this was actually going to work, all the way from how I would walk into their office, to what objections I would raise to the advisors, as well as to how I was going to break it to my parents that my decision was official.

Little did I know that no objection had to be raised, and dropping out was as simple as walking into a room and signing a single resignation paper. Who would have thought that it would have been that easy (Honestly, I am still disappointed about how simple the entire process was because I was ready for a showdown.)?

Nonetheless, it was over.

I had officially joined Bill Gates and Steve Jobs in the entrepreneur-dropout club. I was ready to continue to take on the world, no degree necessary.

The first thing I did after dropping out was go straight to my job site to check on my painters. Unfortunately, an hour after I got back, it started to downpour, and I had to send everyone home. It was probably for the best, though. After all, my mind was now on whether or not I was accepted into the Praxis program.

The anticipation was killing me.

4 p.m., nothing. 5 p.m., nothing.

Then 6 p.m. arrived. I finally received an email from the Praxis director of admissions. I remember I was sitting next to my girlfriend when it arrived, and my hands were shaking.

To me, there was no way that there would even be a chance that I would be denied.

Well, I was wrong…

Fast-forward about eight months, and I received another email from the Praxis team. I had decided to apply one more time, and this time the end result was the opposite. I had made it into the program.

I was ecstatic. However, the reality of the moment was that, although Praxis was a great program, the acceptance notification didn't come at the best timing for me based on where I was in my life.

If there is one thing I regret, it was how I handled the situation of applying to Praxis for the second time (mostly trying to validate myself), getting accepted, and eventually turning down the acceptance. It was a classless move, and I am not proud of it. If anyone from Praxis is reading this, I hope you accept my apology.

So what happened in that eight-month period between the first and second time that I applied to Praxis? How did I set myself up to be continuously exposed to new opportunities?

It's simple. I continued to work hard (of course). But, the real factor was that I continued to leverage risk.

Let me repeat that one more time …

I used risk as leverage and continued to put myself in positions in which success wasn't just one of many options … it was the only option.

I honestly think that the ability to withstand risk is the biggest differentiating factor between immigrants and other people, even more so than the hustle.

I believe that many people work hard, but it's different to have to work hard in a situation where the stakes are high so that you can get back the return that you deserve.

After realizing that I was not accepted into Praxis (the first time I applied), I knew that I had no other option but to completely get the most that I could out of my business, and then use the skills I had learned, the experiences I had learned from, and the results I had obtained during that time to leverage myself into my next opportunity.

Leveraging Risk

I ended up joining forces with Adam Suzor, a young local and successful entrepreneur from Orange, to run the sales and marketing departments at a soon-to-be-gym called Modo. It was yet another risk, and I was more than ready for it.

Adam had started his entrepreneurial journey at a very young age by fixing computers for local residents in town. By the age of 22, Adam had built his company, Suzor IT, into a mini-empire in Orange. He had large contracts with local schools and towns and had developed himself into a success story for the area.

Adam and I connected during the summer, as I would routinely go into his office after long days of work to talk business. We shared a passion for wanting to improve the town that we lived in as well as a passion for helping other small businesses in the area thrive.

An opportunity opened up for me when Adam decided to buy a gym in town. The gym had changed management over three times in the last 10 years. No one had been able to profit off of it, and most of the reason seemed to be because of the area. It was believed that folks in and around Orange didn't have much money, thus the likelihood of the business succeeding there was very slim.

Adam and I disagreed with that belief. We believed that if we were innovative enough, we could figure out a way to bring in enough customers to make the gym profitable. I took on that challenge, and, on October 1st, the first day after I finished painting my last house, ending my summer producing 75,000 dollars' worth of work, I started working to drive clients into the newest gym in town, Modo, as it is still known today.

The risk seemed to pay off in more ways than one. Modo ended up being my playground to continue to develop myself as an entrepreneur. My daily assignment was to figure out how we could bring in more clients. Out of necessity, I developed skills in digital marketing, low-ticket and high-volume sales, copywriting, recruiting high-level talent, and much more. It was a great experience for which I will always be grateful. I stayed with Adam and Modo for about three months, and, in that time period, we were able to gain over 300 clients while also increasing our prices. More importantly, we proved that the locals did have money and were willing to spend it if they found enough value in return (shocking).

I was also able to leverage this experience in order to get even better opportunities not too long after ... another example of using risk as an asset (seems to be a recurring theme here).

By using my knowledge in digital marketing as well as my network and sales experience from my time with Student Painters, I was able to land an opportunity with one of the fastest growing software companies in the world, HubSpot.

The skills I acquired also helped me to land an offer (and eventually an amazing job) with Self-Publishing School. The opportunity for employment with this company, I think, had been an accumulation of all of the previous gambles I had taken during the previous year.

From joining Student Painters, to dropping out of school, to starting a gym, to turning down a great job offer with HubSpot, to going into debt multiple times while investing in different trainings and seminars, my immigrant mentality has helped me ignore those around me and bet on myself, because I realized the potential returns that could come in the future.

The best part? It all started with a gamble taken by my mother, leaving Brazil and coming to the United States. I will never be able to thank her enough for that.

If you could only learn one lesson from immigrants, it should be this: Bet on yourself. Take risks, and the rewards will be so much greater than you ever imagined.

CHAPTER 7

DON'T LISTEN TO REJECTION

My Dream Girl

If I were to list the things that have given me the most joy, I would guarantee that those same things are only a reality in my life because I was able to overcome multiple rounds of rejection to make them a reality.

This is true for both macro situations (getting rejected from the job I now have or the girlfriend I now date), to the micro and more frequent situations, where rejection can literally happen multiple times within the span of an hour (door-knocking or cold-calling).

Rejection fuels me, and I believe that immigrants have an outstanding aptitude for handling rejection. For those of us who made it to a new country, oftentimes we were rejected the first time we tried or rejected from our home country, which turned into the actual reason behind our decision to immigrate in the first place.

The first time my mother and I came into the United States in 2005 (I was seven years old then) our time was cut short because we only had a tourist visa. Six months after moving to a new country, we had to pack our bags and go back to Brazil. This was a pretty disappointing situation for me since I had just started to really pick up English, and my mother had just married my stepfather.

Oh well.

It took us another three years before we were able to get our green cards and move back to the United States. Do you think there was a little bit of overcoming rejection on my mother's end during those three years?

You better believe it.

However, she had a bigger vision for herself and her children, so quitting was never an option.

I am not sure how much that specific situation affected me personally, but after moving to the United States, my ability to take rejection was tested on the first day of fifth grade. I was a little girl-crazy, to say the least, and was definitely not scared to ask for the sale (if you know what I mean). I may have been premature in my class by asking every pretty girl that I met to "go out with me," but that didn't matter. I had the immigrant mindset to keep me going.

Years later as a senior in high school, I found myself in a very similar position as I had been in fifth grade. I'd like to think that my approach with girls had evolved over the years (though my friends may disagree), but nonetheless, I had a girl in mind who I had decided was going to end up being my girlfriend. Of course, I knew that dating was a two-way street. Her feelings had to be mutual. Nevertheless, my mind was set, and I wanted to win her over.

Sound aggressive? It may have been.

She was different from other girls, though. Very different. She "checked all the boxes" and more. Extremely beautiful. Motivated.

Smart as heck (actually graduated number one in our class), and we connected unlike anyone else I had ever talked to before. She was my best friend, and I could see myself with her for a long time. I had to figure out a way to make her my girlfriend.

We started talking a little during the summer before our senior year. I vividly remember that one of our first conversations was about the fact that we had just ordered the same history book at the same time. I ordered it for my own personal reading; she was taking a class that required the book.

We bonded over music, class, our vision for the future. I remember having so many late-night conversations with her, times when I would force myself to stay awake even though I knew that the next morning I would not be very impressed with myself for having done so.

None of that mattered, though, because she made me so happy. For months, all that I hoped was that she felt the same way about me. There was no way that I could see myself being with another girl again.

One of the things I love and hate about myself is that I do not hide things very well. I made it very clear to this girl that I really liked her, and unfortunately, she made it very clear that it wasn't going to happen.

For a few months, you could find me in the deep, dark hole that was "the friend zone." Most think that the friend zone is this inescapable place, that, once you're in it, there is no way out. After a few consecutive months (that's right … months) of talking every single day and dropping not-so-subtle hints about the fact that I wanted to date her, I started to get the feeling that maybe this situation was not going to have a happy ending.

This feeling became even more clear after an away basketball game during our winter break. I was a team captain by that point, and she happened to be the captain of our school's cheerleading team. Even though we weren't dating, she would wait for me outside of the locker room after our games to chat, and on this one night, in particular, I thought that things felt a little different.

Our team had just won a huge game. I personally had had one of my best performances, and we talked just a little longer than usual afterward.

I walked her out to her car, and before saying our final goodbyes, I gave her a hug. After that hug, we looked deeply into each other's eyes, and I asked her if I could kiss her.

I thought that this was finally going to be it, the moment that changed everything between me and the girl of my dreams. But, like most things in life, what happened next did not go according to plan.

She gave me a half-smile and quietly whispered "no," while shaking her head. At that moment, I was convinced that any chance I had of eventually dating her had gone out the window.

My Dream Job

… Two years later, I found myself once again reaching for something that was out of my league.

I first heard about Self-Publishing School and Chandler Bolt during the summer after my freshman year.

I am a huge believer that, whatever you are doing, you should always seek out someone who is doing or has done what you want to do at a higher level. In Student Painters, it was nothing different.

I reached out to many people who were successful in Student Painters, with the goal of both seeing what they did in their painting business and also how they used their experiences to create new opportunities for themselves.

One critical person that I came across is CEO Chandler Bolt, founder of Self-Publishing School.

Chandler was fascinating to me, because, not only did he run a six-figure business with Student Painters, he also dropped out of college for very similar reasons as myself. He was able to build a multi-million-dollar business in a very short time after Student Painters and seemed to be connected with many entrepreneurs whom I admired.

I had to figure out how to get connected to Chandler and at least have a conversation with the guy.

My first move was to do what has been my best networking move to date.

I added Chandler on Facebook and sent him a message explaining who I was and that I would love to have the opportunity to talk with him for 20 minutes about his Student Painters experience.

Chandler did not reply to my message, nor did he accept my friend request. This was very understandable since I knew he was an extremely busy person who valued his time. In fact, he probably didn't even see the message or the friend request.

I didn't have time to get hung up on that, as I had a business to run, for crying out loud. I did, however, slowly start to look more and more into Chandler as well as Self-Publishing School, and both really fascinated me.

I started by listening to Chandler's podcast interviews and reading all of his personal and company articles online. The more I learned about Chandler, the more I knew that I needed to find a way to get close to him. His values aligned with many of my own beliefs, and he was doing exactly what I wanted to do, with a somewhat similar background.

I took no more action toward that goal for a few months. I stayed focused on having a successful summer, and, right after that, I focused on growing Modo. I made sure to keep a close eye on Chandler via social media as well as read a few of his books so I would be ready to act when the opportunity showed itself.

An opportunity indeed came forward. In the middle of November, Chandler announced on our Student Painters Alumni Facebook page that he was hiring a sales representative. By that point, I was heavily invested in Modo, but I was still open to other opportunities if I felt that those opportunities would help me grow faster than I was.

I took action as soon as I saw the post. The problem? I didn't actually know how to actually go about applying for the position.

Chandler had mentioned that he was hiring for the position, but there was no application page to be found. Naturally, my next move was to message him one more time, but that was, once again, unsuccessful.

I had to try something different.

I reached out to a couple of people who knew Chandler and tried getting his email address. I sent a few emails … but no dice.

Then, I had an idea to go completely outside of the box …

If I couldn't get a hold of Chandler, but maybe I could talk with someone on his team. I immediately booked a call to talk with one of his current sales representatives. It was a huge gamble, but worth a shot.

My appointment time was 9 in the morning, and, by 8:55, the nerves started setting in (as they normally do before having what I interpret as high-stakes conversations). At 9 a.m. exactly, I received a call from Lisa, one of Chandler's sales reps.

"Hello? Is this Pedro?" asked Lisa with a tone that made me know that she was not looking to waste any time.

"Yes, this is he. How is it going, Lisa?" I replied.

"Great! So I was just wondering, are you interested in our program, or are you just looking to work with us?" Lisa quickly responded, again showing that she had no time to waste.

"I am actually calling to talk to you about the sales position you are hiring for! I am really interested, and I'm also curious as to how you have been able to succeed in your position? Chandler posted in one of our groups on Facebook, and he mentioned that you are a rockstar and that you are completely crushing it. Do you have 10 minutes right now to tell me about your experience, or would you prefer another time?" I thought that I may have hooked her in by mentioning the fact that I knew she was doing really well in her position.

"So, we don't have sales reps here … " Lisa answered. Not at all what I was expecting.

" … but you can email me three reasons why you think you would be a good fit for our team and three reasons why we should hire you. We can go from there," Lisa said.

Now we were talking!

"Amazing! I will do that right away. Thank you so much, Lisa!" I replied as she quickly hung up.

Boom. Although I didn't really get to talk with Lisa, and I wasn't able to set up a call with Chandler, I did get some next steps. The goal was to really prove myself to Lisa as well as to Chandler. This was a huge challenge, and I was ready for it.

I put a ton of time and effort into writing those emails, making sure I really portrayed characteristics I thought they wanted to see from someone who was going to eventually become part of the team. Along with the email, I also made sure to send in a video that emphasized the areas in which I thought would help me stand out and make a great impression.

Here is the exact email that I sent:

Hello, Lisa,

Thank you SO much for taking some time this morning to talk to me. Before I go further, however, I would like to give you three reasons that make me certain that I would thrive in the Self-Publishing School team, as well as three reasons why I want to join the Self-Publishing School team.

1. Fanatical Work Ethic

I am extremely driven by gratitude and the fact that my mother took the chance to leave her home country of Brazil in order to provide myself and my sister with a better opportunity in America. With that being said, I can say that I have the "immigrant hustle" that will separate myself from other candidates as well as from my colleagues.

This work ethic has been the reason for the accomplishments that I am most proud of, including becoming a two-year-captain for my high school's basketball team (at a monstrous 5'6" frame), running a 75,000-dollar-

revenue painting business (while selling over 120,000-plus dollars' worth of painting jobs), launching a gym with a partner and growing it from zero to 200 members in its first month, and I will be hopefully adding "completely CRUSHING my role at Self-Publishing School" to the list in the near future.

Add to these facts that I do not have a degree and, therefore, expect to be underestimated throughout my career, and the only way that I will get over this fact is by providing more value and completely outworking those in my surroundings. Every. Single. Day.

2. Intellectual Curiosity

Did I mention that I dropped out of school yet? Well, the main reason for this was so that I could continue to educate myself in the areas that I knew were going to be the most beneficial in the long term. Ever since dropping out in May of 2017, I have personally invested in and read over 20 books (both audio and physical copies) in order to learn from geniuses such as Phil Knight, Napoleon Hill, Ray Dalio, Dan Kennedy, Brian Halligan, Gary Hulbert, and more.

On top of that, I can often be found listening to podcasts, such as "The Tim Ferriss Show," "Self-Publishing School," "GaryVee Audio Experience," as well as "Tony Robbins" and other business, sales, marketing, and success-related podcasts.

I have also recently started investing (and thankfully so) in events. Just last month, I was fortunate enough to attend both the Inbound Conference in Boston, as well as the Synergy Global Conference in New York City, and with that I can say that I have seen and learned from Brian Halligan, Richard Branson, Gary Vaynerchuk, Simon Sinek, Michelle Obama, Jordan "The Wolf of Wall Street" Belfort, Malcolm Gladwell, and other world-level performers in business, marketing, and sales.

Currently, I am taking the email marketing certification course through HubSpot Academy, as well as Alex Becker's email marketing course, with the hopes of improving my email/copywriting abilities and using them to start helping the company that I am with, as well as other local entrepreneurs, drive more sales through email. I also recently purchased Grant Cardone's CardoneU and will be using that to continue to improve myself as a salesperson.

Lastly, all of this learning would be useless without application. Fortunately, I have the privilege of applying all that I am learning firsthand in both of the businesses that I am with, Move by Modo (gym), Suzor IT (information technology consulting company), as well as teach all that I learn to new interns at the Young Entrepreneurs Across America, where I teach weekly classes to in the areas of sales, marketing, leadership, and management.

3. I Love the Art AND Science of Sales and Prospecting

Mark Cuban is known for comparing business to sports, and I could not agree more. Business, specifically sales and prospecting, ignites the same adrenaline that I could only compare to my days as an athlete. The process that I went through to master the game of basketball is the same process that I am currently taking to master sales. And the exhilarating feeling that I got by scoring a game-winning basket can only be compared to closing a deal.

The fact that YOU are in the control of your destiny is so liberating because it forces you to develop a whole new level of self-awareness. If you are not succeeding and reaching your goals, the only person to blame is you. I want to be responsible for my outcomes because I am always willing to bet on myself. Sales gave me the opportunity to do that.

* * *

That's enough bragging ... now I want to dive a little deeper into why I believe that Self-Publishing would be a perfect fit for me.

1. The Leadership

I have been following Chandler Bolt ever since this past summer. I actually found out about him because of a podcast that I listened to by Simon Fraser, in which Chandler described his time with the Young Entrepreneurs, his stint in Des Moines, as well as starting Self-Publishing school after his own successes as an author.

During the time, I was in the middle of running my painting business with the Young Entrepreneurs and learning and challenging myself more than ever before. That was also a time in which I was contemplating whether or not I would be going back to school.

Seeing Chandler's success as a college dropout and a Young Entrepreneurs alumni was one of the tipping points that made me realize that the "opportunity cost" of staying in school was way more expensive than even the tuition that I would be paying at the University of Massachusetts. I was also confident enough in myself and knew that, because of my drive and hunger for continuing my education, I would be okay.

Aside from that side story, I honestly believe that Chandler's values, especially the fact that self-improvement is at the top of the list, align with mine. He is a leader that I want to follow and learn from, and I believe that his values have been passed down to the rest of the team as well, and, therefore, I cannot wait to be surrounded by many other like-minded individuals.

2. Mastery

I absolutely love the climb.

I love the process of improving.

I love being forced to step out of my comfort zone.

If I am in an environment where the above factors are true, then I know that I am at the right place.

3. The Mission

"It's not about the book. It's about what the book does for you."

"In going through the process, our students learn a lot about themselves and conquer fears, challenges & limiting beliefs they never knew existed."

What is getting me absolutely FIRED UP right now (even though it is 2:21 a.m.) is the fact that I am writing the email that might position me to begin the process of helping others achieve what the above quotes describe.

I clearly have not felt firsthand the effects that a book can have on someone's life (yet); however, I know that the process, during as well as after releasing a book, can completely change the course of someone's life.

Along with this, I am excited to go to war in the pursuit of putting the publishers out of business. I have no deep-down hate against publishers (maybe I just don't know enough about the industry yet); however, I have a love for empowering the individual.

THAT is what I feel that the Self-Publishing School mission is all about.

Empowering others.

Every day.

Lisa, I am looking forward to speaking with you soon and getting your perspective on what it is actually like to work at Self-Publishing School.

I am also very curious as to how you were able to succeed so quickly in your role. The fact that you so quickly moved on from our call today (or yesterday) showed that you are 100% dialed in and focused. Success leaves clues, and I think I found one from you already.

Thank you again for your time, and I look forward to speaking again.

Good luck and attack the day.

Pedro "Your Future Co-worker" Mattos

Lisa didn't respond as quickly as I wanted after that email, so I sent her another one …

Pedro here, just following up on our last call.

Speaking of follow-up …

As you may know, in most cases, a salesperson will not close on the first interaction.

Close.io CEO Steli Efti even has an article on the power of the follow-up. You can check that out here, it's a great read.

Following up is even more important when you KNOW that you have the solution to a potential lead's problem, yet most get discouraged after they are not answered after the first, second, third, or even fourth attempt.

This past summer, I had a lead with the name of Stanley, and I had to follow up and stop by his house not once, not twice, but eight times.

"I haven't decided yet."

"I'll let you know next week."

"I'm getting other quotes."

Even so, Stanley decided to go in a different direction with his painting needs.

That didn't matter, though, because my philosophy was unless I heard a hard "NO" there was still a chance.

With that being said, I understand that you are busy following a mission, helping customers, and crushing your goals.

However, if it is worth 10 minutes of your time, I would love to set up a call in order to discuss how I could potentially approach the process of becoming a part of the team at Self-Publishing School.

Thank you and I appreciate your time,

Pedro

Boom. After the second email, I finally got a response from Lisa.

I was actually out to dinner with my girlfriend when Lisa sent me the message that I had been waiting five months to receive. She texted me and gave me Chandler's phone number, and I was supposed to call him next weekend.

Finally, the effort had started to pay off. Now, the goal was to be completely dialed in for my follow-up call with Chandler and to prove to him that hiring me would be one of the best decisions he would ever make.

In preparation, I made sure to re-listen to all of his podcasts and read anything by and about Chandler and/or Self-Publishing School that I could find. There was no way that I was going to blow this opportunity.

The day soon arrived, and before I knew it, I was on the phone with the man himself.

After introducing myself, I went right into my story, how I had heard about Chandler, why I was interested in working for Self-Publishing School, as well as what I could bring to the team. We talked for about 45 minutes, and at the end of the conversation, Chandler mentioned he had a few other high-level candidates for the sales position. He asked me when I would be able to start. Thinking that there was really no chance that I would be hired over the other candidates and that I was not yet comfortable leaving Modo, I told Chandler that I would most likely be ready in the spring of 2018. I did, however, follow up by asking Chandler what I could do to prepare for when that time came around, and I was ready to apply again.

His answer was that becoming an actual student of Self-Publishing School and going through the process of writing my own book would be my best bet.

I agreed and soon after became enrolled as an official student of Self-Publishing School.

However, I was fairly disappointed with how the call turned out. It wasn't complete rejection, but I could tell that I hadn't shown all that I could have, and, therefore, Chandler did not think that I would be a good enough candidate to compete with the other people applying for the job.

Bottom line … I was not working for Self-Publishing School, and I needed to do something about it.

The different areas of our lives don't happen in isolation. Your career, your relationships, and your hobbies, all intermingle in some type of way. My point is that, if you start by noticing trends in these different areas, you may learn more about what characteristics are deeply ingrained inside of your character. I wanted to tell these two stories simultaneously to really drive this point home. The way that you approach one thing is the way that you approach everything.

* * *

Ask yourself this question: What would you do if you were faced with rejection from your dream girl or your dream job? Would you take that outcome as permanent, or would you try to change the situation?

How many "no's" can you endure before giving up on what you really want? I can guarantee that the higher the number, the better your quality of life is.

* * *

I have often been told that I have a bad memory. Tests in school that were based strictly on memorizing facts were pretty difficult, and my friends tell me that I often repeat stories, simply because I forget that I told them before.

Growing up, I always thought my bad memory was a flaw. However, it turns out that it is a huge benefit, especially when it comes to overcoming rejection. The ability to very quickly forget about it and bounce back is a skill that I continue to use every time I get a "no." Having a terrible memory allowed me to not be fazed by the fact that the girl of my dreams did not want to date me.

Now, I'm by no means saying that continuing to pursue a girl over and over will be the way that you win her heart. To be honest, I don't know how I was able to change the way she thought about me. All I know is that eventually, it happened.

About four months after the embarrassing situation mentioned earlier in the chapter, the girl of my dreams, Colleen, finally became my girlfriend. We have been dating for over two years as of the publication of this book. I don't think I could have picked a better person as my partner in crime.

* * *

The funny thing about opportunities is that sometimes you have to create them for yourself. That's exactly the approach I decided to take with Self-Publishing School.

After realizing that I was probably not going to be hired as a sales rep right away, I realized that I needed to take a different angle. I knew that if I could provide the company with enough value, they would find a spot for me.

I found my angle once again, after another one of Chandler's posts on Facebook. He was asking his audience how they built their sales teams and what the key components of those teams are.

He soon received a response from Ryan Deiss, CEO of a company called DigitalMarketer.com. Ryan had built the number one resource for digital marketing training on the Internet.

Ryan laid out a simple, yet detailed plan as to how Chandler could build a scalable sales team, incorporating both salespeople (closers) as well as sales development reps (setters). Basically, this single Facebook comment planted the seed in Chandler's mind that maybe he needed a sales development rep. That was a slight opening I knew that I could take advantage of!

I immediately told one of my mentors, Mike Mark, CEO of Netmore.io, about my idea. He quickly sent me some crucial resources that I used to write up a proposal to pitch Chandler the idea of hiring me as the first Sales Development Representative at Self-Publishing School.

I remember devouring a book called *Predictable Revenue* and using what I learned from it to write what ended up being an eight-page sales letter on why Self-Publishing School needed a sales development rep along with why I was the best guy for the job.

About one month after sending that proposal, I had my first official interview. Later that week, on January 3rd, 2018, I was finally offered the job I had been pursuing for over six months.

Six months after all of that, the opportunities that have materialized since have been exponentially greater than what I had envisioned. I've traveled more in the last six months than I have in my entire life, and the best part is that I get paid to do it.

We have started to build out our sales team and have actually hired two more sales development reps in the past couple of months. I have been able to have conversations with some incredibly smart people and have continued learning more about sales, leadership, and overall business every day. I basically get paid to learn from and talk to interesting people. I couldn't have designed a better opportunity for myself if I wanted to.

* * *

The two things that I am most proud of at this moment in life, my relationship and my career, only happened because I was able to overcome massive amounts of rejection during the process.

Immigrants are required to develop the thick skin necessary to handle rejection. It just comes with the environment!

If you take anything out of this book, let it be the fact that being rejected from something you really wanted to have should be all the more reason to keep going after it! Nothing worth having comes easy; therefore, rejection is just a part of the process of achieving the dreams that you have.

Immigrants have been able to figure that out. Have you?

CHAPTER 8

GRATITUDE

How to Guarantee a Life of Misery

How do you continue to overcome rejection while keeping a great outlook on life? I know that, for immigrants, it's all about remembering where we come from and having an immense amount of gratitude for our lives, no matter the current situation.

It's all about perspective.

There is a reason that, after all this time, millions of people every year continue to risk their lives to come to the United States. For those who make it, the power of gratitude for having escaped where they originally came from is more than enough to keep them going during the hard times that follow.

This may be the most powerful lesson out of the entire book. In fact, not learning this lesson will bring you massive consequences. Lack of gratitude may be the biggest cause of unhappiness amongst all the people that I know personally, and I am willing to bet that lack of gratitude is a worldwide epidemic as well.

What I really want to emphasize is what happens when you lack gratitude and how it almost ruined my life.

Here we go.

Although dropping out of school is a decision I am happy that I made, going to college was something I couldn't wait to do.

I was more than ready to leave home and start over in a new place, to meet new people and have experiences that living in Orange wouldn't give me.

One of the best parts about going to UMass was that Colleen, my girlfriend, was going to go as well! The idea of being just a quick walk or bike ride from her sounded like the greatest deal in the world.

I arrived on campus and very quickly began to try to meet new friends. Lucky for me, my roommates and I hit it off pretty quickly. They were both really cool guys who enjoyed sports. I couldn't ask for a better match than that.

The other people on my floor were also extremely friendly people and very easy to talk to. We quickly started grabbing meals and hanging out in our building's common room talking until very late at night.

Everyone also loved a good party.

Naturally, I wanted to see what the party scene in college was all about!

Colleen wasn't a huge fan of parties, so I would go with only friends from my floor. I didn't really party at all in high school, so it was definitely a different experience going to my first frat party. The free alcohol and crazy atmosphere were extremely foreign to me.

The first party I went to was a blast.

I danced, chatted, had a few drinks, and just enjoyed the night with my friends from my floor. After a few hours, we walked back to the dorms, and I crashed having had one of the best experiences yet. The best part is that college had just started.

Though I enjoyed having fun, I was still extremely focused on school, so I wouldn't go out during the weekdays. However, when the following weekend arrived, I was ready to celebrate.

This one particular Saturday morning started out pretty casually. My roommate and I played some late-morning soccer at the local fields at UMass, played some FIFA in the afternoon, and then Colleen and a couple of our friends grabbed some dinner at the local wings place.

At about 11 p.m., I got back to my dorm and was ready to see what the night had in store. It turned out that most of my friends had left, and so we just decided to stay in and play some video games.

What happened in the next couple of hours would prove to be one of the biggest turning points in my life.

After a few games in, Jason started getting tired, and he let me know that he was going to check out for the night. I then decided to head to my next-door neighbor's room to see what she was up to.

After a few minutes, we closed her door, and I went on to make the worst decision that I have ever made.

I had let temptation get the best of me. I broke the trust of the most important person in my entire life. I still can't forgive myself for the decision that stemmed from a lack of gratitude for someone who is nothing short of a blessing in my life. I forgot to be grateful for having a best friend, a partner who was always there to listen to me whenever I needed it. Instead of looking around and saying, "Thank you," I looked around and asked, "What more can I get?"

Unfortunately, expressing gratitude for what we have is extremely uncommon. And that is absolutely the root issue to most people's unhappiness. You truly don't know what you have until it's gone. I ask that you learn this lesson from me as opposed to your own experience. Not because of what may happen to you, but, more importantly, because of what may happen to those around you that are taken for granted.

Colleen and I broke up after that, but we eventually got back together. For a long time, I contemplated whether I should share this story. However, I realized that true transparency is the only way to truly help whoever is reading this book. I believe that one should learn from the mistake of others so you don't have to suffer the consequences yourself.

It's not that I don't think that whoever is reading this will realize that cheating on your significant other is something one should not do. That in itself is obvious and provides no value.

However, the root issue of lacking a sense of gratitude for any aspect of your life is an absolute disease that plagues entire populations.

Most immigrants are lucky enough to have experienced extremely unfortunate situations in their home countries and have an immense sense of gratitude once they have the opportunity to create a new life in a new country, no matter what the circumstances. This one simple trait, more so than any other, is the true reason that immigrants and the children of immigrants succeed to the extent to which they do.

Gratitude gives one the fuel that one needs to apply all the other lessons that I have written about in this book. This is the true superpower of immigrants: the ability to live their lives with gratitude.

CONCLUSION

Life works in cycles. Life happens in seasons.

Events tend to repeat themselves in strange ways.

One of the main reasons why I wrote this book, and I actually didn't realize this until later on, was to hold me accountable. I knew that if I had my personal thesis and beliefs out for the world to see, I would be forced to practice what I preach.

I went to a San Francisco Giants baseball game with Chandler Bolt and one of our friends, Christian. I had spent the previous week working out of Chandler's apartment in San Francisco, with the goal of seeing from up close what made him such a high performer. At that point in my life, I was living with my friends from college still, but I knew that I wanted to start to look for a new place and start over in a new city. After seeing the way that Chandler lived and operated, I realized that he had designed his environment—from the actual city, to his daily routine, to his meals—in a way that was completely optimized to help him achieve his goals.

It was in that moment that I knew that I needed to do the same for myself.

At the game, Christian and I went to the concessions stand to get some chicken tenders. While waiting in line, I started picking Christian's brain on his move from Boston to San Diego, how he enjoyed the new environment, and how that had helped him reach his goals, as I was considering moving to Boston at that point.

Long story short, I was completely sold on the idea of moving to San Diego after that. However, I didn't seriously consider making the move because of the stories I was telling myself about my current situation.

I didn't really know anyone there. I would be too far from my girlfriend and my family. I wouldn't be able to afford it. These thoughts, and every other reason that I could think of at the time, stopped me from seriously considering making the move an option, even though the new network and overall environment I would find myself in would mean a major upside.

Fast-forward one month, and I was in the middle of a 24-hour car ride from Massachusetts to Florida with my girlfriend's family. I had just came off of a nose-to-the-grindstone type of month and was taking a week off to visit my girlfriend's family.

The great thing about long car rides is that you are trapped with your thoughts with nowhere to hide. Whatever is in the back of your mind comes to the surface.

For me, that meant thinking about the possibility of moving to San Diego. The more I thought about it, the more I understood the major positives that would come from the situation, but more limiting beliefs also continued to attack my conscious.

That was until I re-read my manuscript.

I looked over the stories. I meditated on the lessons. And I thought about the decisions that my mother and other immigrants had made when forced to make similar decisions.

Do I risk moving in search of a better and more prosperous life? Or do I stay and play it safe?

Putting it that way … I automatically knew the answer.

Two months later, I packed my bags and started over in the beautiful city of San Diego, California, and this has proven to be one of the best decisions I have ever made.

So what do you do now?

If you have gotten this far in the book, hopefully, you fall into one of the following three categories.

If you are reading this, and you are my mother, I hope that this gives you a better understanding into my story and my values, and I hope that you realized how lucky you are to have experienced all the hardships over the last years. I love you.

If you are reading this and you are either an immigrant or the child of an immigrant, I hope that you realize the great privileges and advantages that you have. Hopefully, you have had experiences that led you to the same realizations. Always remember the sacrifices that were made in order for you to be able to pursue the American Dream. Be eternally grateful no matter how hard life gets, and continue to work hard and make this world a better place.

Now, what about all of you who do not identify yourselves as immigrants? What if you speak one language and you would have to go back many generations to identify your closest non-American ancestor?

Well, here is what I will say.

All of you have had interactions with immigrants in your daily lives. America is a melting pot. Though all of us immigrants have different stories, we also have core similarities that bring us together.

My story is one of millions of other immigrant stories out there, and I hope that you have a better understanding of what drives someone to come to this great country and also how great it is that so many incredible people have made the decision, for themselves and their families, to pursue the American Dream.

Made in the USA
Las Vegas, NV
07 December 2020